What Is an Insect?

By Jenifer W. Day
Illustrated by Dorothea Barlowe

A GOLDEN BOOK • NEW YORK
Western Publishing Company, Inc., Racine, Wisconsin 53404

eggs

This is a housefly.
A housefly is an insect with
    sucking mouth parts.
It has small antennae and big eyes
A housefly has one pair of wings
    and six jointed legs.

maggots

pupa

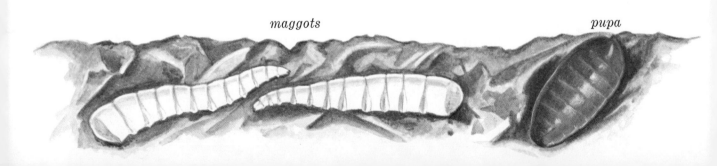

There are many kinds of flies.

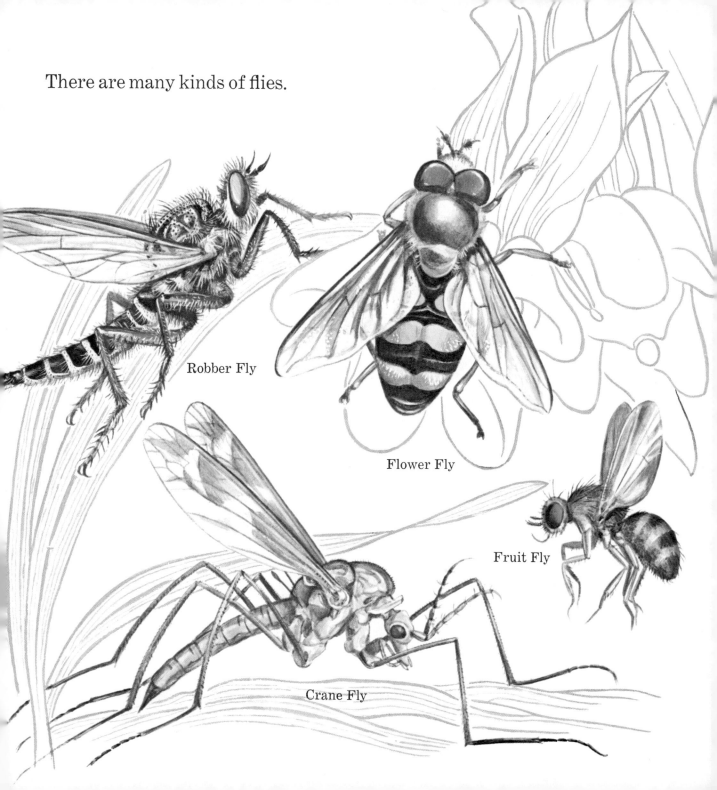

Robber Fly

Flower Fly

Fruit Fly

Crane Fly

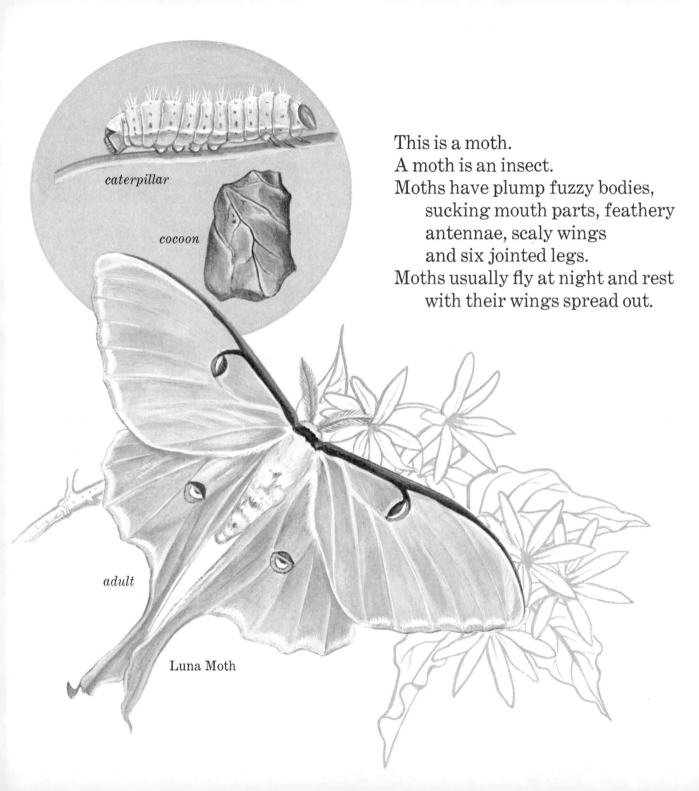

caterpillar

cocoon

This is a moth.
A moth is an insect.
Moths have plump fuzzy bodies,
   sucking mouth parts, feathery
   antennae, scaly wings
   and six jointed legs.
Moths usually fly at night and rest
   with their wings spread out.

adult

Luna Moth

Woolly Bear Moth

Cecropia Moth

There are many kinds of moths.

Io Moth

White-lined
Sphinx Moth

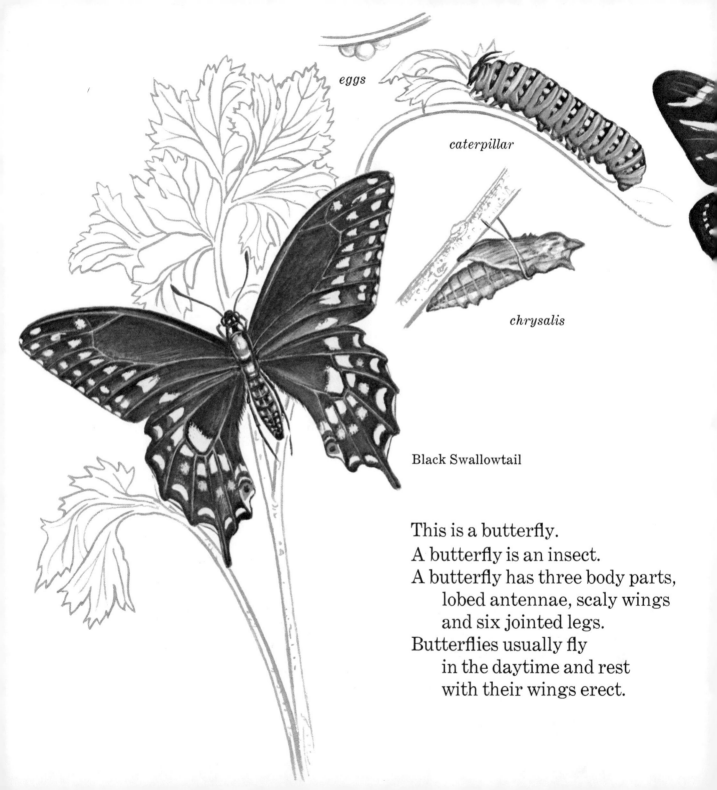

eggs

caterpillar

chrysalis

Black Swallowtail

This is a butterfly.
A butterfly is an insect.
A butterfly has three body parts,
    lobed antennae, scaly wings
    and six jointed legs.
Butterflies usually fly
    in the daytime and rest
    with their wings erect.

Monarch

Zebra

Buckeye

Clouded Sulphur

There are many kinds of butterflies.
Butterflies are related to moths.

Dragonfly

This is a dragonfly.
A dragonfly is an insect.
Dragonflies have long slender bodies,
    short antennae and six jointed legs.
Dragonflies have two pairs of lacy wings
    and are usually found near ponds.

nymph stage

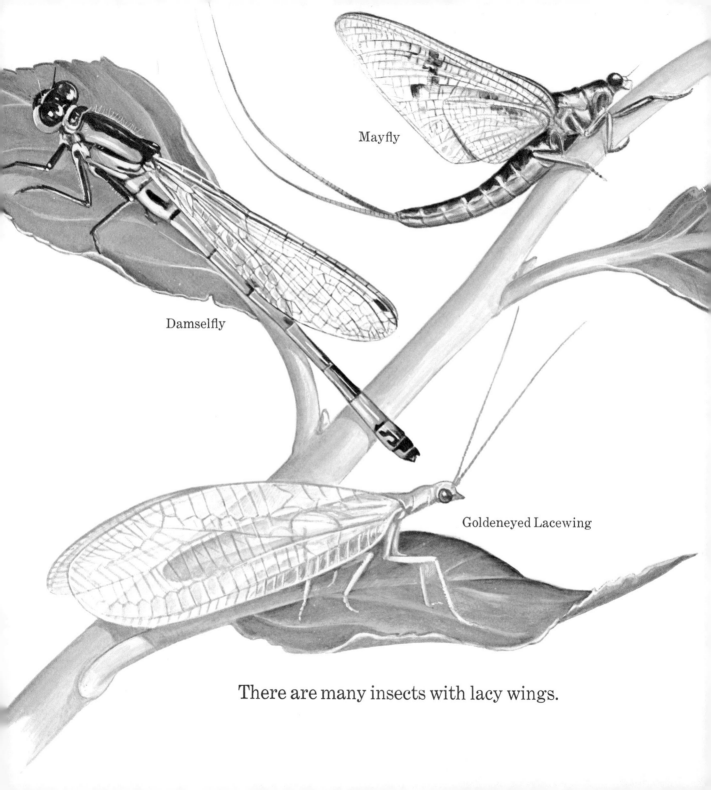

Mayfly

Damselfly

Goldeneyed Lacewing

There are many insects with lacy wings.

This is a grasshopper.
A grasshopper is an insect.
Grasshoppers have three body parts,
    short antennae, chewing mouth
    parts, leathery wings
    and six jointed legs.
Grasshoppers are pests for the farmer
    and food for the birds.

adult laying eggs

nymphs (enlarged)

Grasshoppers have many relatives.

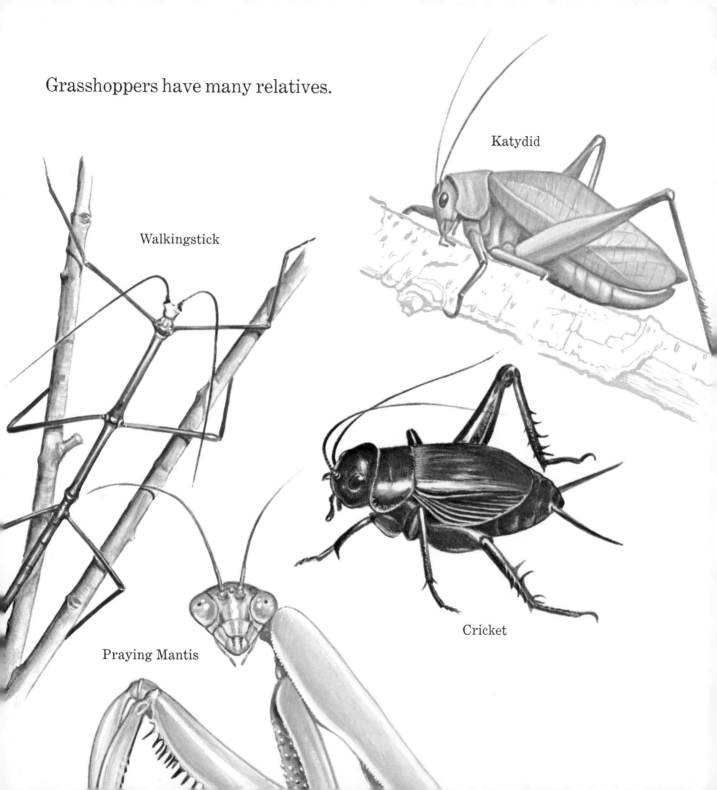

Katydid

Walkingstick

Cricket

Praying Mantis

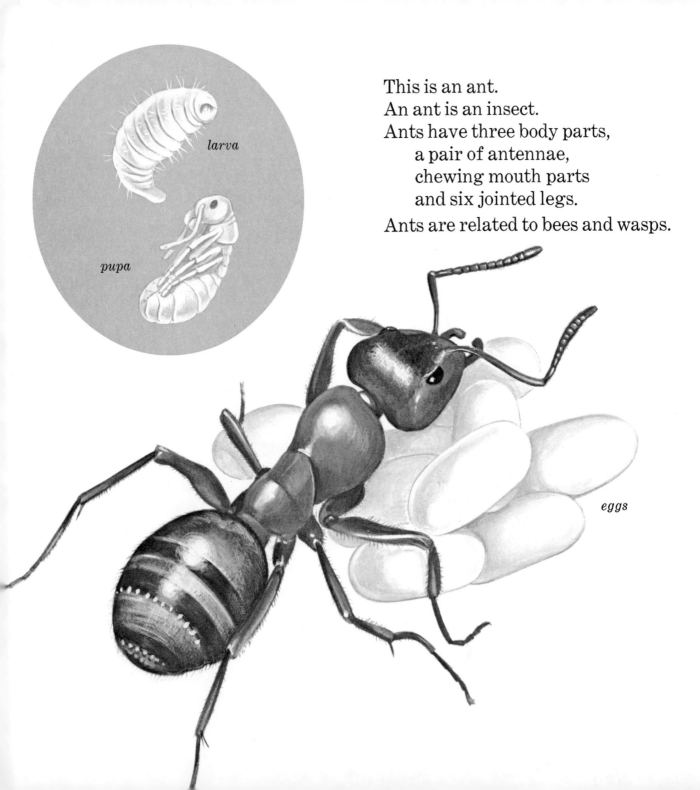

larva

pupa

This is an ant.
An ant is an insect.
Ants have three body parts,
   a pair of antennae,
   chewing mouth parts
   and six jointed legs.
Ants are related to bees and wasps.

eggs

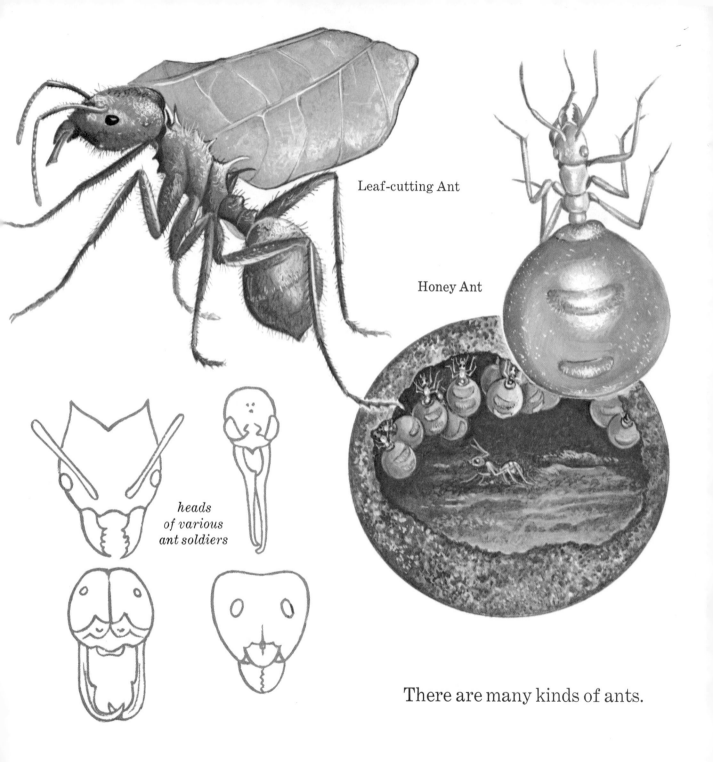

Leaf-cutting Ant

Honey Ant

*heads
of various
ant soldiers*

There are many kinds of ants.

worker

drone (male)

queen

young pupa

eggs

larva ready to hatch

This is a honeybee.
Honeybees are social insects.
They live in colonies and are
  helpful to people.
They make honey and pollinate flowers.
Honeybees have hairy bodies
  and six jointed legs.
They also have stingers.

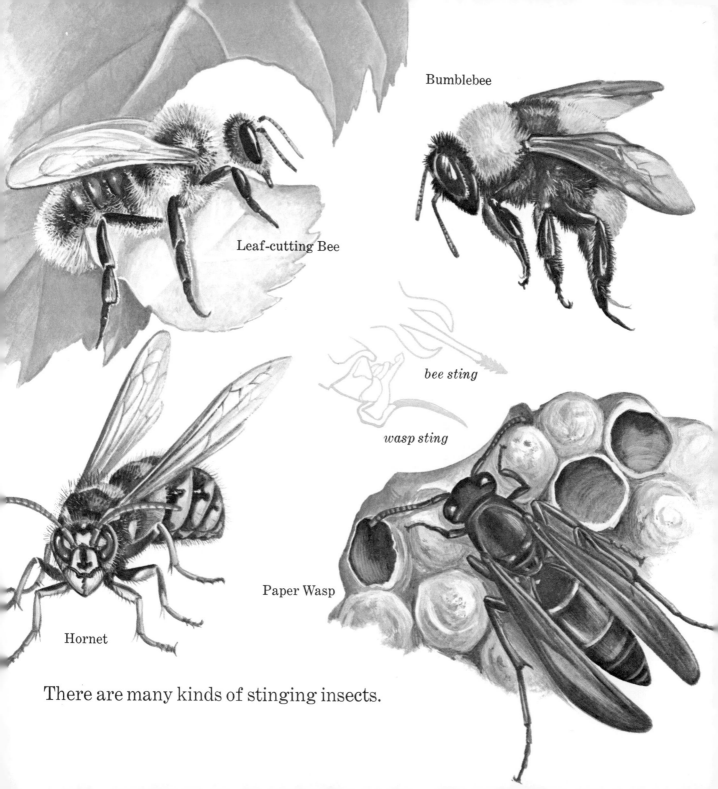

Bumblebee

Leaf-cutting Bee

bee sting

wasp sting

Hornet

Paper Wasp

There are many kinds of stinging insects.

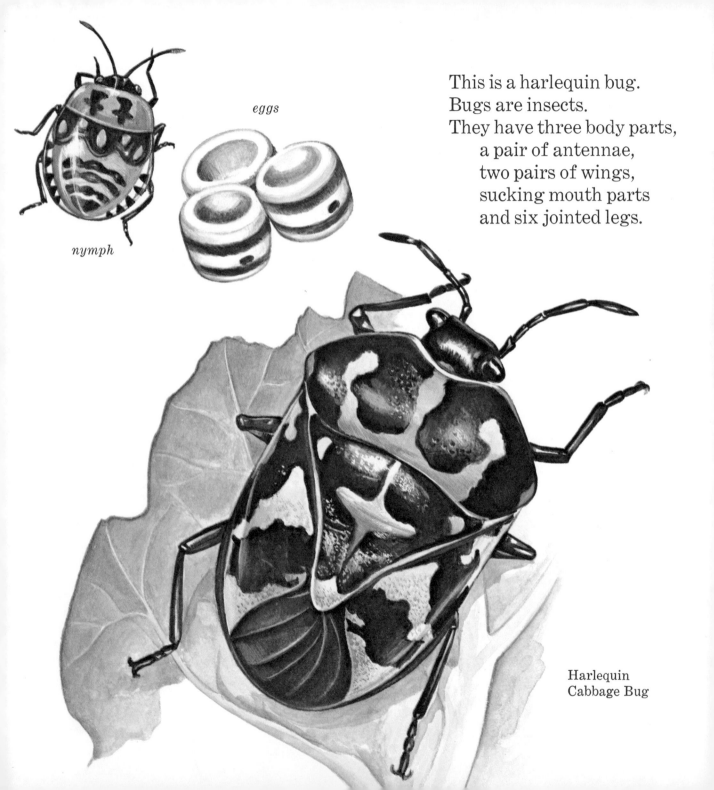

nymph

eggs

This is a harlequin bug.
Bugs are insects.
They have three body parts,
a pair of antennae,
two pairs of wings,
sucking mouth parts
and six jointed legs.

Harlequin
Cabbage Bug

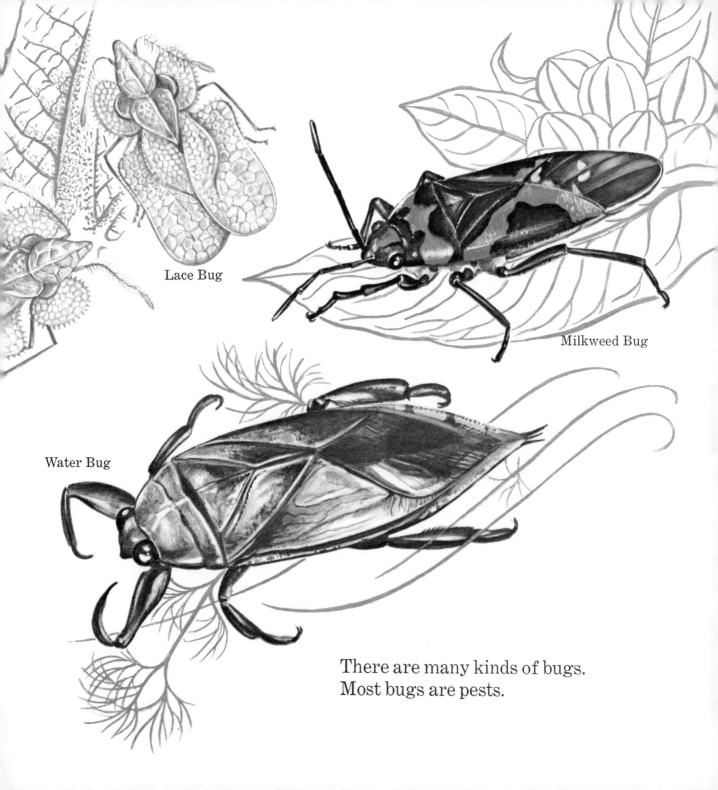

Lace Bug

Milkweed Bug

Water Bug

There are many kinds of bugs.
Most bugs are pests.

This is a June bug.
A June bug is a beetle.
Beetles are insects that have three body parts,
two pairs of wings, short antennae, chewing
mouth parts and six jointed legs.
Some beetles live in water.

June Bug

larva

pupa

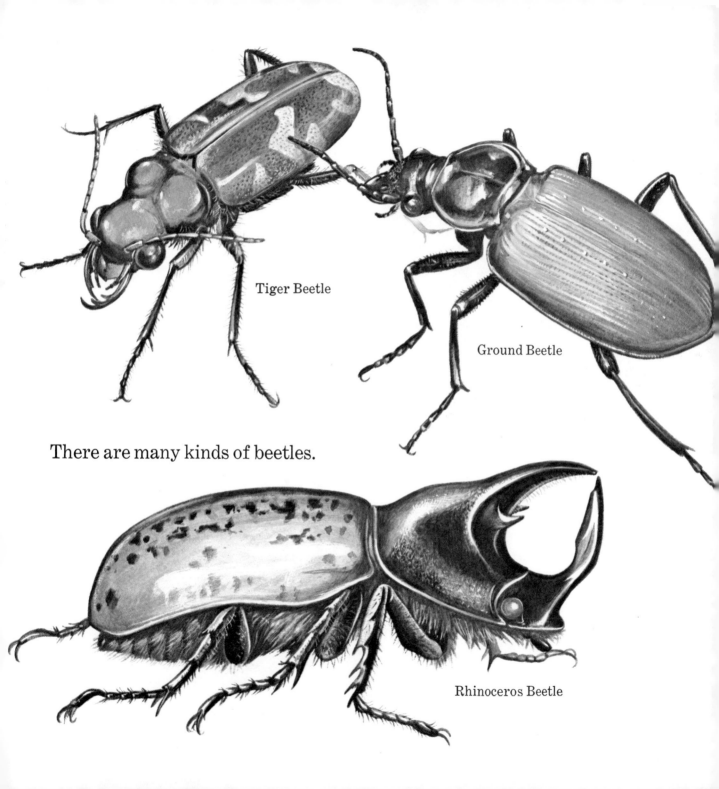

Tiger Beetle

Ground Beetle

There are many kinds of beetles.

Rhinoceros Beetle

*nymph hatching
from egg*

*winged
(summer form)*

wingless female

male

nymph

This is an aphid.
An aphid is an insect.
Aphids are small
    sucking insects that
    feed on plant juices.
They may be winged
    or wingless.

There are many sucking insects
that feed on plant juices.

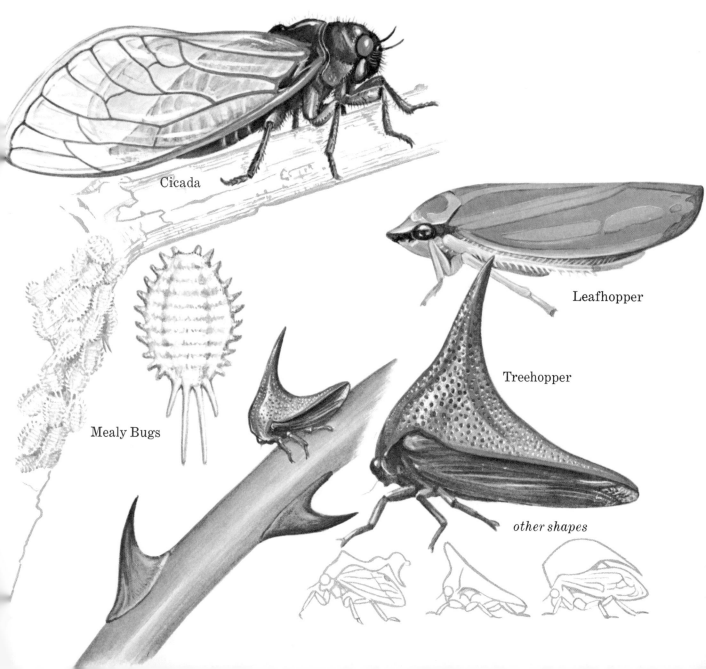

Cicada

Leafhopper

Treehopper

Mealy Bugs

other shapes

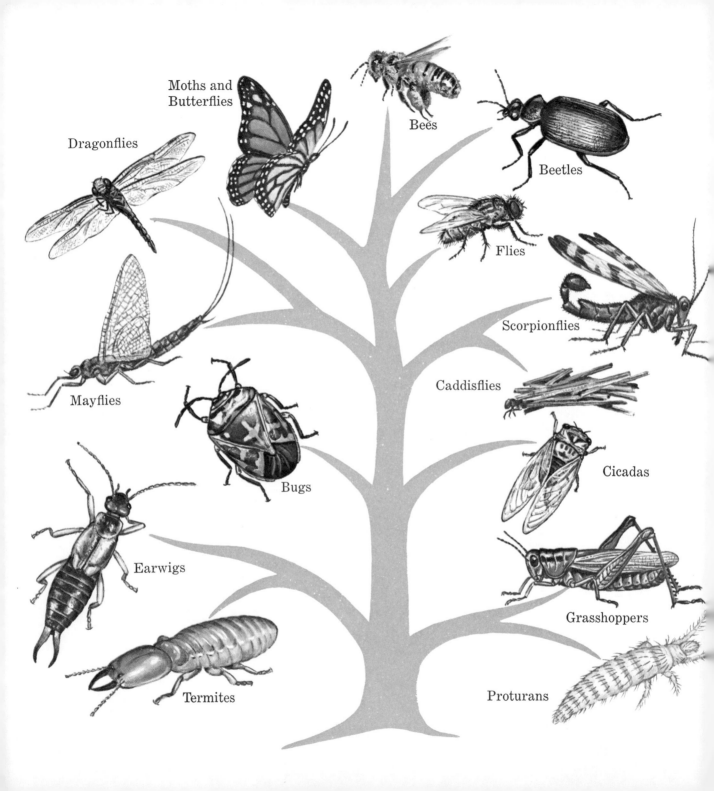

Dragonflies

Moths and Butterflies

Bees

Beetles

Flies

Scorpionflies

Mayflies

Bugs

Caddisflies

Cicadas

Earwigs

Grasshoppers

Termites

Proturans

There are many kinds of insects.

There are biting insects, sucking insects
    and stinging insects.
There are flying insects, crawling insects,
    hopping insects and swimming insects.
There are harmful insects and helpful insects.
There are insects with two pairs of wings
    or one pair of wings,
    and some with no wings.
There are insects with simple eyes
    and compound eyes.
There are many colors of insects
    and insects of many colors.

But what is an insect?

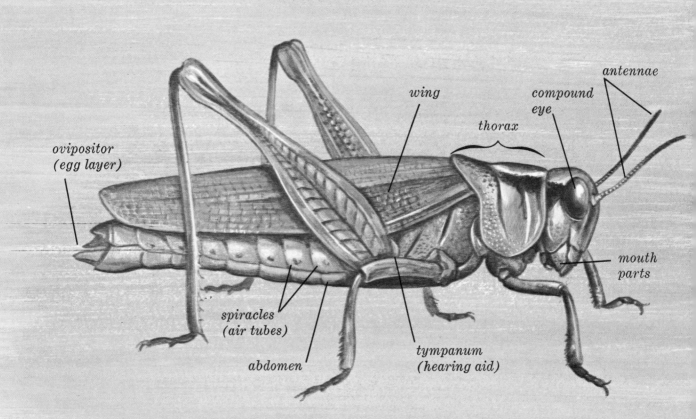

ovipositor
(egg layer)

wing

thorax

compound
eye

antennae

mouth
parts

spiracles
(air tubes)

abdomen

tympanum
(hearing aid)

An insect is an egg-laying animal
     with its skeleton on the outside
     and its muscles on the inside.
A typical insect has three body parts,
     six jointed legs, antennae, and
     usually has wings.
A grasshopper is a typical insect.
There are more than 800,000 different
     kinds of insects.
Insects are among the most fascinating
     creatures in our world.